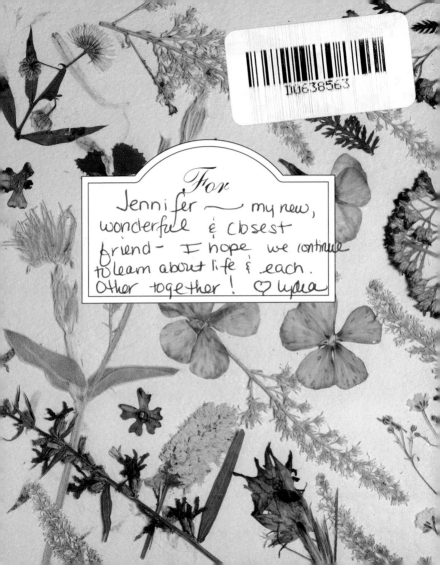

For

Jennifer — my new,
wonderful & closest
friend — I hope we continue
to learn about life & each.
Other together! ♡ Lydia

MOMENTS OF MEDITATION

Inspiration for Daily Living

Edited by Solomon M. Skolnick

Design by Lesley Ehlers
Photographs by Solomon M. Skolnick

PETER PAUPER PRESS, INC.
WHITE PLAINS, NEW YORK

Quotations on double-page art spreads are from
Walt Whitman's *Leaves of Grass*

Pressed flower art by Tauna Andersen
courtesy of Pressed for Time, *Ephraim, Utah*

Copyright © 1995
Peter Pauper Press, Inc.
202 Mamaroneck Avenue
White Plains, NY 10601
All rights reserved
ISBN 0-88088-883-0
Printed in Singapore
7 6 5 4 3 2 1

Index of Contents

Introduction

There is no music in a "rest" but there is the making of music in it.   JOHN RUSKIN

This collection of meditations is organized like a modified book of hours. Twenty-one sets of morning, midday and evening "prayer-stops" provide an easy rhythm to your day. The themes of each set of selections are also presented in the table of contents to afford you variation in the pace of your readings should you wish to move around in the book.

Pause for a moment of meditation. As you read these words let them evolve into private images that nourish you. Be refreshed by your self-awareness and the harmony it brings to you. A renewed sense of balance will allow you to be happy with yourself, and for yourself. Cherish what you feel. It will open your soul to the cosmic.

Morning

Long tresses down to the floor can be beautiful, if
you have that, but learn to love what you have.

ANITA BAKER

Midday

I find that when we really love and accept and *approve of ourselves exactly as we are*, then everything in life works.

LOUISE L. HAY

Evening

I love and accept myself completely as I am.
I don't have to try to please anyone else. I like myself and that's what counts.
I am highly pleasing to myself in the presence of other people.
I express myself freely, fully and easily.
I am a powerful, loving, and creative being.

SHAKTI GAWAIN

LOVE

Morning

I have listened to the realm of the Spirit. I have heard my own soul's voice, and I have remembered that love is the complete and unifying thread of existence.

MARY CASEY

Midday

Love doesn't just sit there, like a stone, it has to be made, like bread; re-made all the time, made new.

URSULA K. LEGUIN

Evening

Love is that vital essence that pervades and per-
meates, from the center to the circumference, the
graduating circle of all thought and action.
Love is the talisman of human weal and woe—the
open sesame to every soul.

ELIZABETH CADY STANTON

I celebrate myself, and sing myself,

And what I assume you shall assume,

For every atom belonging to me as good belongs to you.

ASPIRATIONS

Morning

Far away there in the sunshine are my highest aspirations. I may not reach them, but I can look up and see their beauty, believe in them, and try to follow where they lead.

LOUISA MAY ALCOTT

Midday

The secret of our being is not only to live but to
have something to live for, something towards
which to strive, something to become.

PAUL S. McELROY

Evening

Every year I live I am more convinced that the
waste of life lies in the love we have not given, the
powers we have not used, the selfish prudence
that will risk nothing, and which, shirking pain,
misses happiness as well. No one ever yet was the
poorer in the long run for having once in a life-
time "let out all the length of all the reins."

MARY CHOLMONDELEY

RIGHT RELATIONSHIPS

Morning

The most I can do for my friend is simply to be
his friend. I have no wealth to bestow on him. If
he knows that I am happy in loving him, he will
want no other reward. Is not friendship divine in
this?

HENRY DAVID THOREAU

Midday

One of the most beautiful qualities of true friendship is to understand and to be understood.

SENECA

Evening

I like not only to be loved, but to be told that
I am loved; the realm of silence is large enough
beyond the grave.

GEORGE ELIOT

FAITH

Morning

Kill the snake of doubt in your soul, crush the worms of fear in your heart and mountains will move out of your way.

KATE SEREDY

Midday

We are not human beings trying to be spiritual.
We are spiritual beings trying to be human.

JACQUELYN SMALL

Evening

If it can be verified, we don't need faith. . . .
Faith is for that which lies on the *other* side of
reason. Faith is what makes life bearable, with
all its tragedies and ambiguities and sudden,
startling joys.

MADELEINE L'ENGLE

I do not call one greater
and one smaller,
That which fills its period
and place is equal to any.

PERSPECTIVE

Morning

Every day is a god, each day is a god, and
holiness holds forth in time. I worship each god,
I praise each day splintered down, splintered down
and wrapped in time like a husk, a husk of many
colors spreading, at dawn fast over the mountains
split.

ANNIE DILLARD

Midday

If I love with my Spirit, I don't have to think so
hard with my head.

PEGGY CAHN

Evening

I think that what we're seeking is an experience of being alive, so that our life experiences on the purely physical plane will have resonances within our own innermost being and reality, so that we actually feel the rapture of being alive.

JOSEPH CAMPBELL

LAUGHTER/JOY

Morning

The first thing to be done is laughter, because that sets the trend for the whole day.

OSHO

Midday

The most wasted of days is that in which one has not laughed.

SEBASTIAN R. N. CHAMFORT

Evening

Laughter can be more satisfying than honor; more precious than money; more heart-cleansing than prayer.

HARRIET ROCHLIN

Morning

Can you not see that you must develop? You must have openness of mind—receptivity. Some people are living in pint pots with the covers down. Where are you living?

KATHARINE HINCHMAN NEWCOMB

Midday

I like to think of myself as an artist, and my life is my greatest work of art. Every moment is a moment of creation, and each moment of creation contains infinite possibilities.

SHAKTI GAWAIN

Evening

From the one came two. From the two came the ten thousand things of this world, each of which—from the leaf, to the human, to the planets themselves—having come originally from the one, contains within itself the germ of the original, the life principle . . .

BARBARA ARIA WITH RUSSEL ENG GON

Morning

Before I can take good care of anything or anyone, I must first take good care of my self.

SPENCER JOHNSON, M.D.

Midday

As soon as healing takes place, go out and heal somebody else.

MAYA ANGELOU

Evening

Healing is simply attempting to do more of those things that bring joy and fewer of those things that bring pain.

O. CARL SIMONTON

ASPIRATIONS

Morning

The thing achieved is temporary, but the development of power to achieve is permanent.

LILIAN WHITING

Midday

If you can dream it, you can do it.

WALT DISNEY

Evening

Discovering the ways in which you are exceptional, the particular path you are meant to follow, is your business on this earth . . . It's just that the search takes on a special urgency when you realize that you are mortal.

BERNIE SIEGEL, M.D.

Each of us inevitable,
Each of us limitless—each of us
with his or her right upon
the earth,
Each of us allow'd the eternal
purports of the earth.
Each of us here as divinely as
any is here.

A SENSE OF WHO YOU ARE

Morning

You need to claim the events of your life to make
yourself yours. When you truly possess all you
have been and done, which may take some time,
you are fierce with reality.

FLORIDA SCOTT-MAXWELL

Midday

To do good things in the world, first you must
know who you are and what gives meaning in
your life.

PAULA P. BROWNLEE

Evening

To have the sense of one's intrinsic worth which constitutes self-respect is potentially to have everything: the ability to discriminate, to love and to remain indifferent. To lack it is to be locked within oneself, paradoxically incapable of either love or indifference.

JOAN DIDION

LOVE

Morning

Love is a force. . . . It is not a result; it is a cause. It is not a product. It is a power, like money, or steam or electricity. It is valueless unless you can give something else by means of it.

ANNE MORROW LINDBERGH

Midday

Perhaps loving something is the only starting place there is for making your life your own.

ALICE KOLLER

Evening

If we make our goal to live a life of compassion and unconditional love, then the world will indeed become a garden where all kinds of flowers can bloom and grow.

ELISABETH KÜBLER-ROSS

Morning

Climb the mountains and get their good tidings. Nature's peace will flow into you as sunshine flows into trees. The winds will blow their own freshness into you, and the storms their energy, while care will drop away from you like the leaves of autumn.

JOHN MUIR

Midday

Tranquil pleasures last the longest.

CHRISTIAN BOVÉE

Evening

God grant me the Serenity to accept the things I
cannot change, Courage to change the things I
can, and Wisdom to know the difference.

REINHOLD NIEBUHR

PERSPECTIVE

Morning

Go behind the apparent circumstances of the situation and locate the love in yourself and in all others involved in the situation.

MOTHER TERESA

Midday

There is nothing insignificant—nothing.

SAMUEL TAYLOR COLERIDGE

Evening

To appreciate one does not need to look afar; to be inspired one does not need to have much. In a little jagged stone or small basin, a man may visualize the grandeur of mountains or rivers ten thousand miles long, in a word or a sentence of the ancient sages or worthies, he may read their minds. If so, he has the vision of the noble and the mind of the wise.

TRANSLATED BY CHAO TZE-CHIANG

A Sense of Who You Are

Morning

Don't be ashamed to show your colors, and to own them.

WILLIAM WELLS BROWN

Midday

I expect to pass through this world but once. Any good therefore that I can do, or any kindness that I can show to my fellow-creature, let me do it now.

STEPHEN GRELLET

Evening

Tonight I walk . . . I think of the people who
came before me and how they knew the place-
ment of the stars in the sky . . . Walking, I am
listening to a deeper way. Suddenly all my ances-
tors are behind me. Be still, they say.
Watch and listen. You are the result of the love of
thousands.

LINDA HOGAN

*I see something of God each hour of the
twenty-four, and each moment then,
In the faces of men and women I see God,
and in my own face in the glass,
I find letters from God dropt in the street,
and every one is sign'd by God's name,
And I leave them where they are, for I
know that whereso'er I go,
Others will punctually come for ever
and ever.*

Morning

Joy is prayer—Joy is strength—Joy is love—Joy is
a net of love by which you can catch souls.

MOTHER TERESA

Midday

A good laugh is sunshine in a house.

WILLIAM MAKEPEACE THACKERAY

Evening

The sharing of joy, whether physical, emotional, psychic or intellectual, forms a bridge between the sharers which can be the basis for understanding much of what is not shared between them, and lessens the threat of their difference.

AUDRE LORD

LOVE

Morning

For a love to grow through the tests of everyday living, one must respect that zone of privacy where one retires to relate to the inside instead of the outside.

KAHLIL GIBRAN

Midday

Love is union with somebody, or something, outside oneself, under the condition of retaining the separateness and integrity of one's own self.

ERICH FROMM

Evening

Oh, the comfort, the inexpressible comfort of
feeling safe with a person, having neither to weigh
thoughts nor measure words, but pouring them
all right out, just as they are, chaff and grain
together; certain that a faithful hand will take and
sift them, keep what is worth keeping, and then
with the breath of kindness throw the rest away.

DINAH MARIA MULOCK CRAIK

PERSPECTIVE

Morning

To be really great in little things, to be truly noble
and heroic in the insipid details of every-day life,
is a virtue so rare as to be worthy of canonization.

HARRIET BEECHER STOWE

Midday

The real voyage of discovery consists not in seeking new landscapes, but in having new eyes.

MARCEL PROUST

Evening

Doing work which has to be done over and over again helps us recognize the natural cycles of growth and decay, of birth and death, and thus become aware of the dynamic order of the universe. "Ordinary" work . . . is work that is in harmony with the order we perceive in the natural environment.

FRITJOF CAPRA

SERENITY

Morning

Serenity is active. It is a gentle and firm participation with trust. Serenity is the relaxation of our cells into who we are and a quiet celebration of that relaxation.

ANNE WILSON SCHAEF

Midday

It is tranquil people who accomplish much.

HENRY DAVID THOREAU

Evening

There is, perhaps, no solitary sensation so exquisite as that of slumbering on the grass or hay, shaded from the hot sun by a tree, with the consciousness of a fresh light air running through the wide atmosphere, and the sky stretching far overhead upon all sides.

LEIGH HUNT

FAITH

Morning

No means other than reflection can produce real Spiritual Knowing. Nothing but light can ever reveal the existence of things.

APAROKSHANUBHUTI

Midday

To have faith is to have wings.

JAMES M. BARRIE

Evening

Faith is the substance of things hoped for, the
evidence of things not seen.

HEBREWS 11:2

WISDOM

Morning

The events in our lives happen in a sequence in time, but in their significance to ourselves, they find their own order . . . the continuous thread of revelation.

EUDORA WELTY

Midday

The art of being wise is the art of knowing what to overlook.

WILLIAM JAMES

Evening

Who is wise? He that learns from everyone.
Who is powerful? He that governs his passions.
Who is rich? He that is content.
Who is that? Nobody.

BENJAMIN FRANKLIN

I believe a leaf of grass is no less than the

journey-work of the stars …